ROCK PAINTING GUIDE

Complete step by step guide to learn rock painting skills and techniques with several project ideas

D1706347

Harry Fredrick

Table of contents

CHAPTER ONE

Introduction

Rock painting is an old art form that has grown from its historical origins into a current form of creative expression. "Unearthed Beauty: The Art of Rock Painting" takes you on a trip into the intriguing world of rock painting, where everyday stones are turned into eternal pieces of art. In this introduction, we will look at the historical and contemporary relevance of rock painting, as well as lay the groundwork for a more in-depth look at this engaging art form.

At its foundation, rock painting is beautifying natural stones with a range of patterns, colors, and images. It may range from elaborate patterns and realistic sceneries to abstract artistic interpretations. As we go further into this topic, you'll see that rock painting is about more than simply beautifying stones; it's also about connecting with nature, history, and one's own inner creativity.

Rocks have served as canvases for human expression throughout history. From ancient petroglyphs carved onto cave walls to indigenous peoples' rock drawings, our forefathers have utilized this medium to transmit tales, document events, and express their knowledge of the universe. We'll look at the cultural and historical significance of rock art, as well as how it has left its imprint on the fabric of human history.

The Resurgence of Rock Painting as a Modern Art Form

Rock painting has seen a comeback in popularity in recent years as individuals seek hands-on, creative activities. Painting rocks helps people to escape the rush and bustle of contemporary life by adopting a calmer, more meditative approach to art. We'll look at how this old discipline has been rediscovered and rejuvenated, and how it has found a home in modern art and creative groups.

"Unearthed Beauty: The Art of Rock Painting" allows you to delve into the methods, styles, and inspiration that go into this one-of-a-kind art form. This trip into the world of rock painting will explain how even the most common stones can be turned into magnificent works of art, whether you are a seasoned artist or a novice searching for a creative outlet.

Materials and Tools needed

Rock painting is a fun and easy art form that individuals of all ages and ability levels may enjoy. To make attractive and long-lasting painted rocks, you must first grasp the materials and instruments needed. This part will go over the many sorts of rocks that may be painted, the necessary equipment and paints, and the safety considerations you should take.

The Types of Rocks Suitable for Painting

1. Smooth Surface Rocks: When selecting rocks for painting, smooth surfaces are crucial. Smooth pebbles

provide an excellent canvas for painting because they enable paint to attach more readily and produce a smoother finish. Because of their inherently smooth texture, river rocks and beach stones are good alternatives.

2. Porous Rocks: While smooth rocks are preferable, porous rocks may offer an intriguing texture to your artwork. These pebbles may need more paint to get brilliant colors, but they may provide interesting effects. Porous rocks that may be painted include volcanic rocks and pumice stones.

3. Size and form: The size and form of the rocks you choose might have an impact on the sort of artwork you produce. Smaller rocks are ideal for fine details, whilst bigger rocks provide

more area for complicated sceneries. Experiment with various forms until you discover the perfect canvas for your creative ideas.

4. Local Availability: Consider utilizing locally obtained rocks. This not only connects your artwork to its surroundings, but it also promotes sustainability by avoiding depleting natural resources. If you want to take rocks from natural areas, be sure you have the proper rights.

5. Non-Toxic and Non-Porous: When choosing rocks, be careful. Check if they are non-toxic and non-porous, since certain rocks may contain minerals or compounds that are hazardous when in touch with paint or handled for an extended period of time.

If in doubt, seek the advice of local geologists or specialists.

Essential Tools and Paints

1. Paints: Acrylic paints are the most often used for rock painting. They are available in a broad range of colors, are simple to work with, and cling nicely to rock surfaces. Acrylic paints are

available at craft shops and online. To release your imagination, it's a good idea to invest in a high-quality kit with a variety of colors.

2. Paint Brushes: Fine details and elaborate patterns need the use of high-quality paint brushes. Brushes with diverse tip forms (round, flat, detail) are useful for a variety of painting methods. Experiment with various brush sizes to see what works best for your own style.

3. Sealer: Once you've completed your rock painting, it's critical to preserve it from the weather. A transparent, water-resistant sealer, such as a gloss or matte finish, may help protect and prevent fading of your design. When

your paint is totally dried, apply the sealant.

4. Palette: Whether disposable or reusable, a palette is required for mixing and diluting your paint. To generate specific colors and get the necessary uniformity, you may use a palette made of plastic, glass, or other materials.

5. Water and a Cloth or Paper Towel: You'll need water to clean your brushes and thin paints between color changes. Always have a cloth or paper towels on hand to blot brushes and repair errors.

6. Pencils and Erasers: Use these to sketch out your design before you begin painting. To verify your measurements and arrangement are

perfect, lightly sketch your ideas on the rock's surface.

7. Stencils and Decals: If you're not comfortable painting freehand, stencils and decals may help you create exact shapes and patterns on your rocks.

8. Paint Palettes and Containers: Use containers to mix bespoke colors or to store paint for later use. Small paint palettes or pill organizers work well for this.

Safety Precautions for Rock Painting

1. Ventilation: Always work with acrylic paints in a well-ventilated location. Although acrylic paints are usually harmless, enough ventilation may aid in the dissipation of any fumes.

2. Safety Equipment: While acrylic paints are non-toxic, it's a good idea to wear old clothes or a smock to protect your clothes. If you're worried about getting paint on your skin, use disposable gloves.

3. Child Safety: If children are participating in rock painting, keep a constant eye on them, particularly while they are handling paints and tiny materials that might constitute a choking danger. Teach kids about hand hygiene and how to handle art products properly.

4. Clean-up: Clean up any paint spills or splatters as soon as possible to avoid sliding or trailing paint into unexpected places. Dispose of paint

and cleaning supplies in accordance with local requirements.

5. Health Considerations: If you have any known sensitivities or allergies to certain art products, check the labels carefully and choose suitable materials. Seek medical attention if you have any harmful effects.

6. Nature Respect: If you take rocks from natural areas, do it carefully and ethically. Follow local norms and standards, and avoid disturbing local ecosystems.

You may go on your artistic adventure with confidence if you understand the supplies and instruments needed for rock painting and take the necessary safety measures. With the necessary supplies in hand, you're ready to explore the world of rock painting's numerous methods and styles.

CHAPTER TWO

Getting Started

Rock painting is a creative and rewarding art form that anybody can enjoy, but it does need a few preliminary tasks. In this part, we'll go over how to start your rock painting adventure, from locating the correct rocks to cleaning and prepping their surfaces, and lastly, selecting the perfect design or seeking inspiration for your masterpiece.

Choosing the Right Rocks

1. Natural vs. Purchased Rocks:

o Natural Rocks: Collecting rocks from your surroundings may be a fun activity. These pebbles may have distinct forms and textures that offer dimension to your creation. Natural rocks for painting may be found in beaches, riverbanks, and hiking routes.

o Store-Bought Rocks: Smooth, pre-selected rocks may also be purchased from craft shops or internet vendors. Store-bought pebbles are often more regular in shape and size, making them appropriate for certain projects or themes.

2. Size and Shape: o Size: The size of your rock will have an impact on the intricacy of your design. Smaller rocks are ideal for fine work, whilst bigger rocks provide greater area for complex sceneries or various pieces. When deciding on the size of your rocks, keep the aim of your artwork in mind.

o Shape: Different forms might spark creative thoughts. Landscapes and abstract patterns benefit from flat, oval-shaped rocks. Rocks with irregular shapes may indicate more organic or realistic patterns.

3. Texture and Color: o Texture: Smooth rocks are often used for painting since they give a good canvas for intricate work. Porous rocks, on the other hand, may be utilized to produce fascinating textural effects, albeit they may take more paint to get brilliant colors.

o Color: The colors of natural rocks may compliment or improve your design. Consider if the current colors of the rock will complement your selected design, or whether you will need to prepare the surface by painting a base coat.

4. Ethical and Local Collection: o Always follow local legislation and norms when gathering natural rocks. Be attentive of the environment and ecosystems, and avoid causing harm or disruption to natural environments. Some places have limits on rock gathering, so do your homework ahead of time.

Surface Cleaning and Preparation

1. Cleaning Rocks: o Thoroughly clean your rocks before you begin painting. The surfaces of natural rocks are often covered with dirt, debris, or oils. Scrub lightly with a soft brush or toothbrush and soapy water to clean them. Before beginning to paint, thoroughly rinse the pebbles and allow them to dry fully.

2. Sanding and Smoothing: o If your rocks have rough areas or

abnormalities, use fine-grit sandpaper to smooth them out. This step might assist you in achieving a uniform surface and improved paint adherence.

3. Base Coat: o Depending on the color and texture of your rock, a base coat may be required. A white or light-colored base coat may enhance the vibrancy of the colors in your pattern. Allow the base coat to fully dry before moving on.

4. Priming: o Consider using a primer for more sophisticated or complex paintings. A primer may improve the adhesion of the paint to the rock and provide a smoother surface for complex motifs. Allow the primer to dry completely after applying it.

5. Base Coat Sealing: To improve the longevity of your base coat, consider sealing it with a transparent acrylic sealer. This will keep the base coat from combining with the future coats of paint.

Choosing the Right Design or Seeking Inspiration

1. Create Your Own: One of the most enjoyable aspects of rock painting is the fact that you have unlimited creative freedom. You may create your own artwork from the ground up. Begin by drawing your design on paper and transferring it to the surface of the rock using a pencil.

If you're new to rock painting, start with basic designs. To begin, consider geometric patterns, abstract forms, or inspiring quotations.

o As your confidence and skill grow, you may go on to more complicated drawings like as animals, landscapes, or portraits.

2. Nature as a source of inspiration: o Nature is a great source of inspiration for rock painting. Painting animals, flowers, landscapes, or seascapes are all options. Each natural feature provides a distinct and visually beautiful backdrop for your rocks.

o Nature-themed rock paintings may serve as reminders of the outdoors' splendor, making them ideal for garden or outdoor décor.

3. Themes and Seasons: o Create themed rock art to celebrate the changing seasons. For instance, in the spring, you may paint flowers and

bright colors, and in the fall, you could paint autumn leaves and cozy settings.

o Holidays like Halloween, Christmas, and Easter provide opportunity to make themed rock art to commemorate the occasion.

4. Inspirational Quotes and sentiments: o Adding words to your rock art may express inspirational and positive sentiments. Paint quotations, affirmations, or encouraging messages on your rocks. These might be inspiring for both you and people who see your work.

o Think about the message's goal, whether it's for personal encouragement, as a present, or to share positive in the community.

5. Replicating legendary Artwork: o Rock painting gives a unique platform for mini-masterpieces if you want to recreate legendary artwork on a tiny scale. You might try to imitate famous painters' classic works or styles from different art groups.

6. Collaborative Projects: o Group rock painting projects are a great way to bring people together. Encourage friends, family, or the local community to join you in a collaborative effort in which everyone contributes to a broader, unified design.

o Collaborative initiatives may be utilized to raise funds, raise awareness, or involve the community.

7. Seeking Inspiration Online: o The internet is a fantastic source of

inspiration for rock painting. Visit websites, social media platforms, and rock painting forums to view a diverse range of designs done by other painters.

oRock painting ideas and methods are often included in galleries on Pinterest, Instagram, and Facebook groups.

Remember that there are no precise restrictions when it comes to rock painting; it's all about releasing your creativity and unique expression.
You're ready to start your rock painting journey with the correct rocks in hand, a clean and prepared surface, and a well-thought-out design or inspiration. Experiment, enjoy yourself, and let your creative path emerge naturally.

CHAPTER THREE

Rock Painting Inspired by Nature

Nature has traditionally been a source of great inspiration for artists. It has a wide range of topics, colors, and textures that may be nicely transferred onto a rock canvas. Nature-inspired rock painting is a popular topic that enables artists to connect with their surroundings in a meaningful manner while also celebrating the beauty of the natural world. In this part, we'll look at many elements of nature-inspired rock painting.

1. Fauna and Flora

Flora and animals are a popular motif in nature-inspired rock painting. The forms, colors, and textures of flowers, plants, and animals are often sources of inspiration for artists. Among the suggestions are:

• Flowers in the wild: Colorful, detailed blooms may be painted on your rocks. Each flower may be considered a little work of art, capturing the delicate petals and vibrant colors.

• Butterflies and Birds: Make a sequence of pebbles with different attitudes of butterflies or different types of birds. These topics are ideal for displaying vivid and complex details.

• Marine Life: Because the ocean is filled with life, it offers an abundant source of inspiration. On your rocks, paint seashells, starfish, seahorses, or even elaborate aquatic sceneries.

• Animals: From cherished pets to spectacular wildlife, animals provide limitless opportunities for rock painting. You may make realistic depictions as well as stylized, creative interpretations.

2. Scenery and Landscapes

You may also use rock painting to capture the beauty of natural landscapes and sceneries. On your rocks, you may draw calm sunsets, rough mountains, lush forests, and quiet lakes. These landscapes may provide a feeling of calm and closeness to nature.

• Sunsets and Sunrises: Use your pebbles to paint the vibrant colors of the sky at dawn or sunset. Tree or animal silhouettes may lend depth and interest to these settings.

• Mountains and Hills: Use textured, layered patterns to capture the magnificence of mountains and hills. You may even create three-dimensional effects by layering paint.

• Seascapes: Use rugged beaches, crashing waves, and coastal plants to depict the ever-changing character of the sea. To add depth and movement to your seascapes, use a range of blues and greens.

3. Weather and Seasonal Themes

Seasonal and weather cycles provide a dynamic source of inspiration for nature-themed rock painting. You may make a succession of pebbles to symbolize each season or concentrate on certain weather conditions.

The Four Seasons: Use your rock drawings to explore the beauty of spring, summer, autumn, and winter. Use seasonal elements such as blooms, falling leaves, or snowfall.

• Rainbows: After a storm, a rainbow may represent hope and beauty. Paint dazzling rainbows on your rocks with their vivid variety of colors.

• Rain and Storms: To depict the drama of a thunderstorm, use dark, melancholy colors. The visual contrast between dark clouds and dazzling lightning may be stunning.

4. Nature and Inspirational Quotes

Quotes and messages reflecting the fundamental link between people and the natural environment are often included in nature-inspired rock art. Including words on your pebbles may increase the emotional effect of your work.

• Nature quotations: To go with your nature-themed artwork, choose quotations from prominent naturalists, poets, or environmentalists. These quotations might help to strengthen the meaning of your artwork.

• Affirmations that are positive: Incorporate positive affirmations and encouraging statements into your nature-inspired rock art. Those that come into contact with your work may find it inspiring.

Abstract and Contemporary Styles

In contrast to nature-inspired rock painting's meticulous and accurate features, abstract and modern styles provide a more fluid and creative approach to the art form. Abstract rock painting provides for several interpretations and forms of artistic expression. Let's look at some features of abstract and modern rock art.

1. Abstract Geometry

For individuals who desire a structured and contemporary appearance, geometric abstraction is a common alternative. Shapes, lines, and patterns are used to create visually appealing designs on rocks.

• Mosaic Designs: Create a mosaic-like look on the rock's surface by arranging geometric shapes such as squares, triangles, or circles in complicated patterns.

• Optical Illusions: Play around with geometric shapes to create optical illusions. These patterns may deceive the observer, making your rocks more interesting and lively.

• Color Blocking: Strong visual impact may be achieved by arranging opposing colors in geometric designs. Consider employing complimentary colors to create patterns that are lively and eye-catching.

2. Abstraction of Fluids and Organics

A more free-form approach, fluid and organic abstraction often depends on the artist's intuition and inventiveness. It values organic, flowing lines and forms that aren't restricted by rigorous geometric restrictions.

• Fluid forms: Use your creativity to create organic forms and patterns that flow smoothly over the surface of the rock. This technique often imitates the natural curves and contours of the rock.

• Blended Colors: Use gradients and color mixing to add depth and movement to your abstract designs. The shift from one color to another may generate a visually appealing effect.

• Abstraction Inspired by Nature: Use organic shapes and colors inspired by nature to combine the abstract and nature-inspired styles. This might result in a balanced combination of rigidity and mobility.

3. Modern Themes and Pop Art

Modern culture, fashions, and pop art may all serve as sources of inspiration for contemporary rock painting. These designs are frequently whimsical, vivid, and visually powerful, reflecting the contemporary zeitgeist.

• Pop Culture allusions: Draw pictures of prominent pop culture people, symbols, or allusions on rocks. These rocks might be a fun and nostalgic method to reach out to modern consumers.

• Abstract Pop Art: Incorporate aspects of abstraction and pop art into your designs by employing vivid colors, simple forms, and a lively, comic-book-style approach.

• Symbols and Typography: Use current typography and symbols to express modern messages and thoughts. You may use words, emoticons, and symbols from social media and technology into your designs.

4. Collage and mixed media

Mixed media and collage methods may also be used in contemporary rock painting. This entails creating texture and depth using materials other than paint.

• Collage Components: Attach tiny, textured items to your rocks, such as cloth, paper, or beads, to create tactile and visually intriguing artworks.

• Include Natural Elements: Combine natural components with your artwork, such as twigs, leaves, or shells. This marriage of nature and modern art may produce one-of-a-kind and thought-provoking works.

5. Simplicity

The essence of minimalist rock painting is simplicity and reduction to the fundamentals. These designs often use a restricted color palette and emphasize clean lines, forms, and negative space.

• Monochromatic Color Scheme: To achieve a feeling of simplicity and elegance in your rock paintings, choose a single color or a limited color pallet.

• Negative Space: Allow the natural color of the rock to peek through as part of the design. To achieve a visually balanced arrangement, leave areas of the rock unpainted.

Finally, nature-inspired rock painting and abstract/contemporary styles provide painters with a diverse range of options. Nature-themed paintings connect with the natural world's beauty, yet abstract and contemporary forms allow for experimentation and modern expression. Rock painting is an art style that invites creativity and self-expression, whether you prefer to immerse yourself in the nuances of nature or journey into the infinite worlds of abstraction. The decision between both methods is ultimately determined by your particular hobbies, mood, and creative vision, and you may even blend components from both

to create a genuinely unique approach
to rock painting.

CHAPTER FOUR

STONE PAINTING PROJECTS

Guide to painting Mandala Stones

Mandala stone painting is a relaxing and peaceful rock painting activity. Mandalas are circular designs that radiate from a center point. To create your own mandala stone, follow these steps:

Materials You will require:

1. A smooth and clean rock (choose a size that matches your needs).

2. Acrylic paints in a variety of colors.

3. Various sizes of fine paintbrushes (for intricate work).

4. A color pallet for combining.

5. A pencil or chalk for basic design drawing.

6. A cup of water and paper towels for washing brushes.

7. A transparent acrylic sealant to preserve your completed mandala.

Step 1: Get Your Rock Ready

To begin, thoroughly clean your rock with soap and water to remove any dirt or residue. Allow it to totally dry. To produce a smoother painting surface, sand any rough areas or inconsistencies in your rock using fine-grit sandpaper.

Step 2: Draw the Center

Draw a little circle in the middle of the rock using a pencil or chalk. This will be the starting point for your mandala creation. You may also create a basic pattern inside the middle, such as a little dot or a smaller circle.

Step 3: Design the Primary Elements

Begin by choosing a design element for your mandala's initial layer. Popular shapes include flowers, dots, and teardrops. Begin in the middle and work your way outward. Take your time and be careful to maintain consistent spacing and symmetry. Allow one color to dry for this layer.

Step 4: Include Detail Layers

Continue to add design components in layers, spreading outward from the center. Each layer might have a different design element or color. You may keep the same part or try out other designs. It is critical to maintain symmetry while making a balanced mandala. For finer details, a smaller brush might be used.

Step 5: Keep Symmetry

Maintain symmetry by rotating the rock frequently while you work on your mandala. This guarantees that your design is balanced from all perspectives. Take your time and pay attention to details to create a visually beautiful mandala.

Step 6: Personalize and Experiment

Feel free to add your own personal touches to your mandala. Try out various patterns, colors, and shapes. The beauty of mandala painting is that there are no hard and fast restrictions, enabling you to express yourself freely.

Step 7: Finishing Touches

Take a step back and evaluate your work when you've finished your mandala design. Make any necessary revisions if there are any flaws or places that need improvement. Touch up lines and details using a fine brush.

Allow to Dry in Step 8

Allow your mandala stone to fully dry before moving on to the next stage. This guarantees that your design is preserved.

Step 9: Finish Your Mandala

Apply a transparent acrylic sealer on your mandala to preserve it from wear and the weather. Use the sealer according to the manufacturer's directions. Typically, many thin coats should be applied, with each coat drying before applying the next. This will keep your mandala looking fresh and safe.

Step 10: Showcase and Enjoy

Your mandala stone is now finished and ready to display. You may put it in your garden, on your windowsill, or as a nice and homemade present. The complex patterns and brilliant colors of the mandala will provide beauty and peace to any home.

Remember that making mandala stones may be a relaxing and peaceful activity. Allow your imagination to flow organically and don't hurry the process. You'll become better at creating and painting elaborate mandalas on rocks as you practice.

Guide to painting superman logo on rocks

For admirers of the renowned superhero, painting the Superman insignia on a rock may be a fun and creative endeavor. Here's a step-by-step method to getting there:

You will need the following materials:

1. A smooth and clean rock (of the appropriate size for your design).

2. Red, yellow, and black acrylic paints (or blue if you like the original Superman colors).

3. delicate paintbrushes, one of which is for delicate details.

4. A color pallet for combining.

5. A pencil or chalk to doodle the logo.

6. A cup of water and paper towels for washing brushes.

7. A transparent acrylic sealer to preserve your completed logo.

Step 1: Get Your Rock Ready

To begin, thoroughly clean your rock with soap and water to remove any dirt or residue. Allow it to totally dry. If your rock has rough areas or imperfections, you may smooth out the painting surface with fine-grit sandpaper.

Step 2: Draw the Superman logo.

Draw the basic outline of the Superman logo on the rock using a pencil or chalk. Begin with the famous "S" form, which is made up of two mirrored "S" curves.

Step 3: Paint the Background of the Logo

Start by painting the backdrop in the Superman logo's trademark color to make it stand out. The backdrop is often yellow, although some versions utilize blue. Allow a solid application of the selected color to dry.

Step 4: Apply the "S" Symbol.

When the backdrop is dry, gently paint the "S" sign with red paint. Begin with one "S" curve and then repeat on the other side. Make sure the curves are smooth and symmetrical. Take your time in order to create a clean and clear design.

Step 5: Include Specifics

To add the complex features to the "S" sign, use black paint. Begin by defining the form by outlining the edges. Then draw the diagonal lines within the "S." Make sure these lines are equally spaced since they will create a grid pattern.

Step 6: Tweak the Logo

Examine your painted logo and make any required changes or touch-ups.

Make sure the lines are clean and the design is balanced.

Step 7: Let it Dry

Allow your Superman logo rock to fully dry before moving on to the next stage. This is necessary to avoid smudge or color mixing.

Step 8: Embroider Your Superman Logo

Apply a transparent acrylic sealant to preserve and extend the life of your painted Superman logo. Use the sealer according to the manufacturer's directions. You may need to apply many thin layers, letting each coat to dry before proceeding.

Step 9: Show Off Your Superman Logo

Your Superman logo rock is now finished and ready for display. You may display it on your desk, in your superhero memorabilia collection, or even in your garden as a one-of-a-kind piece of outdoor décor.

Making a Superman emblem out of rocks is a unique way to honor this beloved character. Feel free to play around with other logo versions or tweak it to your liking. You may produce a crisp and colorful rendition of the Man of Steel's symbol on a rock with practice.

Rock critters guide on painting ladybug on rocks

Making ladybug rock creatures may be a fun and creative pastime. To paint ladybugs on rocks, follow these simple steps:

Materials You will require:

1. Clean, smooth pebbles (select rocks that are the right size for your ladybug).

2. Red, black, and white acrylic paints.

3. delicate paintbrushes, one of which is for delicate details.

4. A color pallet for combining.

5. A pencil or chalk to draw the ladybug.

6. A cup of water and paper towels for washing brushes.

7. A transparent acrylic sealant to keep your final ladybug rock safe.

Step 1: Get Your Rock Ready

Begin by scrubbing your rock thoroughly with soap and water to eliminate any dirt or debris. Allow it to dry fully. If your rock has any rough spots, you may smooth them off with fine-grit sandpaper before painting.

Step 2: Draw the Ladybug

Sketch the basic contour of the ladybug on the rock using a pencil or chalk. Begin with a rounder form for the torso and a smaller, oval shape for the head. Make room for the ladybug's markings, wings, and face.

Step 3: Apply a base coat to the Ladybug.

Carefully paint the ladybug's body with red acrylic paint. To create a strong, brilliant red color, you may need to apply additional coats. Allow each coat to dry completely before applying the next.

Step 4: Paint the Ladybug's Head With black acrylic paint, paint the ladybug's head (the smaller oval form you drew previously). Leave a tiny piece of the face unpainted at the front.

Step 5: Include Spots

It's now time to add the ladybug's distinctive markings. Make a series of circular dots on the red body using black paint. Ladybugs normally have seven to twenty-one spots, which may vary in layout. Feel free to experiment with the quantity and placement of spots.

Step 6: Make a Face

Make the ladybug's face out of white paint. Two tiny white circles are used for the eyes, and a white "C" shape or semicircle is used for the mouth or "smile." You may add small black dots for the eyes to give additional realism.

Step 7: Finishing Touches

Apply minute details to the ladybug's spots, eyes, and face using a fine paintbrush and black paint. This stage will bring your ladybug to life by defining the attributes.

Step 8: Antennas and Legs

Add six small black lines on either side of the body for the ladybug's legs. These lines should be spaced uniformly and placed along the body's margin. In addition, add two black antennas to the ladybug's head.

Allow to Dry in Step 9

Allow your ladybug rock to dry fully before moving on to the next stage.

This is necessary to guarantee that the paint dries and does not smear.

Step ten: Finish Your Ladybug Rock

Apply a transparent acrylic sealant to preserve and extend the life of your painted ladybug. Use the sealer according to the manufacturer's directions. You may need to apply many thin layers, letting each coat to dry before proceeding.

Step 11: Show Off Your Ladybug Rock

Your ladybug rock critter is now finished and ready for display. You may put it in your yard, on a windowsill, or use it as a charming house decoration. These adorable ladybug pebbles make excellent presents or garden markers.

Ladybug rock critters are not only a fun and creative activity, but they are also a great way to bring a bit of nature-inspired art to your surrounds. You may paint ladybugs on rocks with brilliant colors and exquisite features with experience, making each ladybug unique and intriguing.

CHAPTER FIVE

Guide on painting fish on rocks

Painting fish on rocks is a fun and artistic activity. To make your own fish-themed rock art, follow this step-by-step guide:

Materials 1. A clean, smooth rock (choose a size and shape appropriate for your fish design).

2. Various colored acrylic paints (for the fish, water, and backdrop).

3. Various sizes of fine paintbrushes (for detailing and filling in bigger areas).

4. A color pallet for combining.

5. A pencil or chalk to draw the fish.

6. A cup of water and paper towels for washing brushes.

7. A transparent acrylic sealant to keep your final fish rock safe.

Step 1: Get Your Rock Ready

Begin by properly washing your rock with soap and water to eliminate any dirt or debris. Allow it to totally dry. If your rock has rough spots or abnormalities, use fine-grit sandpaper to smooth off the surface before painting.

Step 2: Draw Your Fish

Draw the outline of your fish on the rock using a pencil or chalk. Begin with the body form, fins, and tail of the fish. You may use reference photographs or draw your own styled fish.

Step 3: Apply the Base Coat on the Fish

Choose a foundation color for your fish and use acrylic paint to gently paint its body. Allow the initial layer to dry before adding further coats to obtain a solid and brilliant color. For complete coverage, you may need to apply two or more coats.

Step 4: Attach the fins and tail of the fish.

Paint your fish's fins and tail with the right colors. For precise sections, use a small brush, and for bigger fins, use a larger brush. The quantity and form of fins you paint will be determined on the sort of fish you're painting. Check that the fins and tail are distinct and symmetrical.

Step 5: Create the Eye

Paint the fish's eye using a little brush or the tip of a fine brush. Consider using a contrasting color for the iris and adding a little white accent to make the eye seem more natural.

Step 6: Finish the Scales

Add scales to your fish to give it a textured and realistic look. Simple brushstrokes in a pattern that follows the curves of the fish's body may be used to make these. To give the scales dimension, choose a slightly distinct shade or color.

Step 7: Water and Background

Consider if you want to provide your fish with a water habitat. If this is the case, paint the background appropriately. You may indicate water by using blue or green tones, or you can opt for a more abstract backdrop. Allow the fish to dry before beginning the background.

Step 8: Finishing Touches and Highlights

Make any extra features, such as lines, patterns, or shading, to your fish. You may also add highlights to the body of the fish to make it look more three-dimensional. These details may help your fish seem more realistic.

Allow to Dry in Step 9

Allow the painted fish and backdrop to fully dry. This is necessary to guarantee that the paint sets and does not smear when the sealer is applied.

Seal Your Fish Rock in Step 10

Apply a transparent acrylic sealant to your painted fish to preserve it and extend its life. Use the sealer according to the manufacturer's directions. Typically, numerous thin coatings are required, with each coat drying before applying the next.

Step 11: Show Off Your Fish Rock

Your fish rock painting is now finished and ready to display. You may use it as a beautiful element for your house, on a shelf, or in your garden. Fish-themed pebbles may also be offered as presents to friends or family members who admire your creative abilities.

Making fish-themed rock art is an excellent way to combine your love of nature with your creative abilities. With experience, you can paint vivid, intricate, and visually attractive fish on rocks, making each fish unique and engaging.

Guide to making owl painted rocks

Crafting attractive, nature-inspired décor with owl painted pebbles is a fun and creative pastime. To make your own owl rocks, follow the steps below:

You will need the following materials:

1. Clean, smooth pebbles (in sizes and shapes appropriate for your owl designs).

2. Various colored acrylic paints for the owl and backdrop.

3. Various sizes of fine paintbrushes (for detailing and filling in bigger areas).

4. A color pallet for combining.

5. A pencil or chalk to draw the owls.

6. A cup of water and paper towels for washing brushes.

7. A transparent acrylic sealant to keep your final owl rocks looking good.

Step 1: Gather Your Stones

Begin by properly washing your rocks with soap and water to eliminate any dirt or debris. Allow them to totally dry. If your pebbles have rough areas or inconsistencies, smooth them up with fine-grit sandpaper before painting.

Step 2: Draw Your Owls

Draw the outline of your owl on the rock using a pencil or chalk. Begin with the form of the owl's body, head, wings, and tail. You may either utilize reference photographs or design your own stylized owl.

Step 3: Apply an Owl Base Coat.

Choose a foundation color for your owl and use acrylic paint to paint its body. Allow the initial layer to dry before adding further coats to obtain a solid and brilliant color. You may need to apply two or more coats depending on the size of your owl.

Add the Owl's Facial Features in Step 4

Draw the owl's face, including the eyes, beak, and talons. Owls have huge, expressive eyes, so draw elaborate eye patterns with a delicate brush. Highlights and features in the eyes provide depth and authenticity.

Step 5: Apply paint to the wings and tail.

Color the owl's wings and tail using acrylic paint. You may either use reference photographs for certain owl species or create your own color palette. Make sure the wings and tail are well defined and detailed.

Step 6: Feather Specifics

Use a small brush to add features like streaks and lines radiating outward from the eyes to resemble the feel of owl feathers. These strokes will create the appearance of soft, fluffy feathers. For the feather details, use a slightly different shade of the base color or a lighter color.

Step 7: Scenery and Background

Consider if you want to use your owl rocks to create a backdrop or landscape. This may provide an additional layer of visual intrigue. You may, for example, paint a moon, stars, trees, or any other natural environment you like.

Step 8: Finishing Touches & Highlights

If you've made a scene, add any more elements to your owl rocks, such as tree branches or leaves. Highlights may also be added to the owl's body to make it look more three-dimensional. These details add to the realism of your owls.

Allow to Dry in Step 9

Allow your owls and background to dry fully. This is necessary to guarantee that the paint sets and does not smear when the sealer is applied.

Seal Your Owl Rocks in Step 10

Apply a transparent acrylic sealant to your painted owl pebbles to preserve them and extend their life. Use the sealer according to the manufacturer's directions. Typically, numerous thin coatings are required, with each coat drying before applying the next.

Step 11: Show Off Your Owl Rocks

Your owl-painted rocks are now finished and ready to display. You may use them as wonderful ornamental items on a windowsill, in your yard, or in your house. These owl-themed pebbles also make excellent presents for wildlife and art lovers.

Creating owl-painted pebbles is a unique way to combine nature and art. With experience, you may paint vivid, realistic, and visually attractive owls on rocks, making each owl unique and charming.

Guide to making snowman painted rocks

Making snowman painted rocks is a fun and creative hobby to do during the winter season. To build your own snowman rocks, follow these steps:

You will need the following materials:

1. Smooth, clean pebbles (different sizes for different snowmen).

2. Acrylic paints in white, black, orange, and any other colors you like for accessories.

3. Detailing and filling in bigger sections with fine paintbrushes.

4. A color pallet for combining.

5. A pencil or chalk to draw the snowman.

6. A cup of water and paper towels for washing brushes.

7. A transparent acrylic sealant to keep your final snowman rocks protected.

Step 1: Gather Your Stones

To begin, thoroughly clean your rocks with soap and water to remove any dirt or debris. Allow them to totally dry. If your pebbles have rough areas or inconsistencies, smooth them up with fine-grit sandpaper before painting.

Step 2: Draw Your Snowmen

Draw the outlines of your snowman on the rocks using a pencil or chalk. Begin with the snowmen's bodies, heads, and any additional accessories, such as scarves, hats, or mittens.

Step 3: Apply a base coat of paint to the snowman.

White acrylic paint should be used to paint the snowmen's bodies and heads. Allow the first coat to dry before applying the second. Depending on the size of your snowman, two or more coats may be required to obtain a strong, vivid white color.

Paint the Snowman Faces in Step 4

Paint the snowmen's eyes, lips, and buttons with black paint. Detail with a fine brush. Create little, irregular forms to lend individuality to snowmen, which generally feature coal or stone-like eyes and mouths.

Step 5: Finish with an Orange Carrot Nose.

Add iconic carrot-shaped noses to your snowmen using orange paint. Carrot noses are usually triangular or conical in shape. For a whimsical touch, make tiny, basic shapes.

Step 6: Adorn Your Snowmen

Add scarves, hats, and mittens to your snowmen to make them more unique. Make each snowman unique by using different colors. To add character, paint stripes, dots, or designs on the accessories.

Step 7: Paint the buttons and arms

If you want your snowmen to have arms, draw thin, curving lines from the sides of their bodies. You may also use black paint to add more buttons along the fronts of the snowmen.

Step 8: Finish the Faces

To add features to the snowmen's faces, use a fine brush and black paint. Pink or red dots may be used to produce rosy cheeks. To add depth and luster to the eyes and buttons, highlight them.

Allow to Dry in Step 9

Allow your painted snowman to dry fully before applying the sealant to ensure that the paint settles and does not smear.

Seal Your Snowman Rocks in Step 10

Apply a transparent acrylic sealant to preserve and extend the life of your painted snowman rocks. Use the sealer according to the manufacturer's directions. Typically, numerous thin coatings are required, with each coat drying before applying the next.

Step 11: Show Off Your Snowman Rocks

Your snowman painted rocks are finished and ready to display. Put them on a windowsill, mantel, or in the yard, or use them as festive holiday decorations. Snowman rocks also make lovely presents for friends and family, giving a whimsical touch to their holiday décor.

Making snowman painted rocks is a creative and enjoyable way to celebrate the winter season. With experience, you may paint snowmen on rocks with personality and charm, making each snowman distinctive and charming.

CHAPTER SIX

How to Make Laughing Emoji on Rocks

Making a laughing emoji out of a rock is a creative and enjoyable hobby. To paint a laughing emoji on a rock, follow these steps:

Materials You will require:

1. A clean, smooth rock (of the appropriate size and form for your design).

2. Yellow, black, and white acrylic paints (for the emoji's face characteristics).

3. Detailing and filling in bigger sections with fine paintbrushes.

4. A color pallet for combining.

5. A pencil or chalk to draw the emoji.

6. A cup of water and paper towels for washing brushes.

7. A transparent acrylic sealant to keep your completed rock safe.

Step 1: Get Your Rock Ready

To begin, thoroughly clean your rock with soap and water to remove any dirt or debris. Allow it to totally dry. If your rock has rough areas or imperfections, smooth them down with fine-grit sandpaper before painting.

Step 2: Draw the Laughter Emoji.

Draw the outline of your laughing emoji on the rock using a pencil or chalk. Begin with the round face form.

Step 3: Apply the Base Coat.

To make the emoji's face, use a bright yellow acrylic paint. Allow to dry after carefully painting the circular form. You may need to apply two or more coats depending on the size and color intensity you prefer.

Paint the Facial Features in Step 4

Add the emoji's face characteristics using black and white acrylic paint.

Begin by painting the eyes, which are often oval or almond in form. To produce a sparkling impression, leave a little white highlight in each eye. To depict the laughing, paint a curving, open-mouthed grin for the mouth.

Step 5: Make the eyes more detailed.

Make black pupils for the eyes using black paint. To highlight the emoji's laughing, draw little curved lines at the corners of the eyes to show that they are closed or almost closed.

6th Step: Highlights and Shadows

Highlight the eyes and lips with a thin brush and white paint. These accents provide definition to the emoji's characteristics, making it look more three-dimensional. To produce delicate shadows around the eyes and lips, use a very diluted black or gray.

Step 7: Let it Dry

Allow your laughing emoji rock to fully dry before moving on to the next stage. This is necessary to guarantee that the paint sets and does not smear when the sealer is applied.

Step 8: Put a Stamp on Your Laughter Emoji Rock

Apply a transparent acrylic sealant to your painted laughing emoji rock to preserve it and extend its life. Use the sealer according to the manufacturer's directions. Typically, numerous thin coatings are required, with each coat drying before applying the next.

Step 9: Show Off Your Laughter Emoji Rock!

Your painted laughing emoji rock is now finished and ready to be displayed. You may put it on your desk, in your yard, or as a bright house decoration. Laughter emoji rocks are also great presents for friends and family who appreciate your creative sense of humor.

Making a laughing emoji rock is a fun and creative hobby that will offer a sense of comedy to your surrounds. With practice, you can paint emojis on rocks that encapsulate the pleasure of laughing and make people who see them smile.

Guide to painting happy birthday on a rock

A creative and customized way to honor a significant occasion is to write a "Happy Birthday" inscription on a rock. To paint "Happy Birthday" on a rock, follow these steps:

Materials You will require:

1. A clean, smooth rock (choose a size and form appropriate for your message).

2. Various colored acrylic paints for the phrase and backdrop.

3. Detailing and filling in bigger sections with fine paintbrushes.

4. A color pallet for combining.

5. A pencil or chalk to scribble the message.

6. A cup of water and paper towels for washing brushes.

7. A transparent acrylic sealant to keep your completed rock safe.

Step 1: Get Your Rock Ready

To begin, thoroughly clean your rock with soap and water to remove any dirt or debris. Allow it to totally dry. If your rock has rough areas or imperfections, smooth them down with fine-grit sandpaper before painting.

Step 2: Draw a "Happy Birthday" message.

Sketch the "Happy Birthday" inscription on the rock softly using a pencil or chalk. Layout and spacing should be planned to ensure that your message is centered and visually pleasing.

Paint the Message Base Coat in Step 3

Choose a bold color for the "Happy Birthday" message. Using acrylic paint, carefully paint the message's letters. For this phase, a fine brush is recommended. Allow the first coat to dry before applying the second. You may need to apply two or more coats depending on the size of your message and the color intensity you prefer.

Step 4: Create a shadow or outline

Consider adding a shadow or outline in a contrasting color to make the message stand out. If your base coat is light, for example, choose a deeper color for the shadow or outline. This adds depth and makes the message stand out.

Step 5: Create a Background

You have the option of making a backdrop for your "Happy Birthday" greeting. Paint the area surrounding the message in a complimentary color. This will draw attention to the message. Allow the message to dry fully before painting the backdrop.

Step 6: Hone the Message

Once the message and backdrop are dry, tidy up the edges and do any required touch-ups with a fine brush. Make sure the letters are tidy and distinct.

Step 7: Let it Dry

Allow your "Happy Birthday" message rock to fully dry before moving on to the next stage. This is necessary to guarantee that the paint sets and does not smear when the sealer is applied.

Step 8: Finish Your Rock

Apply a transparent acrylic sealant to your painted "Happy Birthday" rock to preserve it and extend its life. Use the sealer according to the manufacturer's directions. Typically, numerous thin coatings are required, with each coat drying before applying the next.

Step 9: Optional Personalization and Decorating

You may add ornamental components such as balloons, cake, or flowers to further customize your birthday rock. Use diverse colors and forms to make the design colorful and one-of-a-kind.

Step 10: Show Off Your Birthday Rock

Your "Happy Birthday" painted rock is finished and ready to display. Put it on a windowsill, in your yard, or as part of a birthday party centerpiece. Personalized birthday pebbles are especially thoughtful and unique presents for friends and loved ones on their big day.

A sincere and unique way to commemorate someone's birthday is to write a "Happy Birthday" greeting on a rock. With experience, you may paint vivid, visually attractive birthday greetings on rocks that are loaded with loving wishes.

Ideas for Showcasing Rock Art

Rock art is a varied and creative method of self-expression, and displaying your painted rocks may be just as inventive. There are countless methods to display your masterpieces, whether you're painting rocks for leisure, giving, or as a sort of outdoor decorating.

A. Indoor Exhibits:

1. Shelves or Shadow Boxes: Place your painted pebbles on shelves or

within shadow boxes. This results in a well-organized and visually beautiful display that enables you to edit and rearrange your rock art as needed.

2. Table Centerpieces: Arrange your rocks in a pretty tray or dish and use them as table or mantel centerpieces. This offers a splash of color as well as a personal touch to your home design.

3. Gallery Wall: Make a gallery wall by putting your painted rocks on a wall in a grid or irregular design. To firmly connect the pebbles while allowing for simple rearranging, use sticky putty or hooks.

B. Garden Stones: Arrange your painted rocks carefully in your garden or outdoor places. These stones may be used as garden markers, ornamental accents, or as part of a rock garden plan.

2. walkway Stones: Turn your painted pebbles into walkway stepping stones. This gives your garden or yard a fun and customized touch.

3. Rock Towers or Cairns: Build attractive towers or cairns out of your rocks. These may be eye-catching focus pieces for your outdoor areas.

C. Exchange and Hiding of Rock Art:

1. Rock Art Hunts: Take part in the popular practice of exchanging rock art. Paint a series of pebbles, conceal them throughout your neighborhood, and challenge people to discover them. Attach a label with instructions for re-hiding or exchanging the rocks for the finders.

2. Social Media and Online forums: Post photos of your painted rocks on social media and in online rock art forums. Connect with other rock musicians and share ideas and inspiration.

3. Rock Art Workshops or exhibits: Plan or attend rock art workshops and exhibits. This gives you the chance to show off your work to a larger audience and interact with other artists.

How to Keep Painted Rocks Safe from the Elements

Preserving the brilliance and durability of your painted rocks is critical to guaranteeing their longevity, particularly when placed outside. Consider the following methods to safeguard your painted rocks from the elements:

A. Capping:

• Acrylic Sealants: Seal your painted rocks with a transparent acrylic sealant. These sealers are available in a variety of finishes, including gloss, satin, and matte, and give protection against moisture, UV radiation, and fading. Use the sealer according to the manufacturer's directions.

• Apply many thin coats of acrylic sealer to increase protection. Allow each coat to completely dry before applying the next. This forms a strong barrier against the elements.

B. Proper Rock Selection: • Smooth and Non-Porous Rocks: Select smooth and non-porous rocks. These pebbles are less prone to absorb moisture, which may cause paint breaking and fading over time.

• Sealed Bases: If you want to use rocks as garden markers or outside décor, consider sealing the bottom with a waterproof sealer. This protects the rock from moisture and soil contact even further.

• Covered regions: When exhibiting painted rocks outside, consider displaying them in regions that are shaded from bright sunshine and heavy rains. This limits your exposure to severe weather.

• Raised Garden Beds: If you're going to use rocks as garden markers, make sure they're in raised garden beds or containers. These create a regulated environment and prevent direct soil and moisture contact.

D. Periodic Maintenance: • Inspect on a regular basis: Check your painted rocks for indications of wear and tear on a regular basis. Consider resealing or repainting the rocks if you see any damage or fading.

• Reapply Sealer: The protective sealer may wear off over time. Reapply a transparent acrylic sealer to your painted rocks once a year or as required to preserve protection.

• Off-Season Storage: If you use painted rocks as seasonal decorations, consider keeping them within during the off-season to keep them safe from the weather.

• Temperature Control: Keep your rocks in a consistent indoor climate to avoid dramatic temperature variations that might cause cracking or paint damage.

Rock Painting's Therapeutic and Meditative Aspects

Rock painting may be a therapeutic and contemplative exercise that provides a variety of physical, mental, and emotional advantages. Here's a more in-depth look at the therapeutic benefits of rock painting:

A. Stress Reduction: • awareness: Because rock painting demands concentrated attention on the present moment, it promotes awareness. Painting helps people to divert their attention away from worries and totally immerse themselves in the creative process.

• Relaxation: Participating in creative activities such as rock painting causes the release of dopamine and endorphins, which may contribute to feelings of relaxation and stress reduction.

B. Self-Expression and Creativity: • Artistic Expression: Individuals may express themselves artistically and emotionally via rock painting. Even individuals who may not consider themselves artists might find an outlet for their creativity and self-expression via it.

• Empowerment: Finishing a painted rock may provide a feeling of achievement and empowerment, which can be particularly beneficial for those coping with low self-esteem or self-doubt.

C. Concentration and Focus: • Concentration Skills: Rock painting involves concentration, attention to detail, and hand-eye coordination. Such exercises may increase focus and cognitive abilities.

• Stress Reduction: Painting rocks offers a distraction from nervous or intrusive thoughts, allowing people to focus on a useful and fun work.

D. Meditation and Mindfulness:

• Meditative mood: Because rock painting is repetitive and rhythmic, it may generate a meditative mood. Painting rocks becomes a type of meditation for many artists, resulting in calm and mental clarity.

• Stress Relief: Mindful and contemplative hobbies such as rock painting have been related to stress reduction, reduced blood pressure, and general well-being.

E. Community and Connection:

• Social Bonding: Rock painting is popular as a communal activity. As artists share their creations, conduct seminars, or engage in rock art exchange events, it encourages social relationships.

• Emotional Support: Rock painting may give emotional support as well as a feeling of belonging. During difficult times, such as the COVID-19 epidemic, communities often band together to help one another.

• Coping with Trauma: For some people, rock painting acts as a coping method while dealing with trauma, sorrow, or traumatic life events. During difficult circumstances, the procedure may be therapeutic and provide a feeling of control.

• tension Reduction: Painting rocks may be a fun method to relieve tension and anxiety. It provides a creative outlet as well as a feeling of achievement, which contributes to emotional well-being.

Finally, rock painting is a therapeutic and contemplative activity as well as a creative and artistic pursuit. It has a variety of physical, mental, and emotional advantages, such as stress reduction, self-expression, greater attention, and a feeling of camaraderie. Painting rocks, whether you're a seasoned artist or a novice, may be a truly satisfying and enlightening experience that adds to your entire well-being.

Made in United States
Troutdale, OR
04/08/2025

30459938R00060